For Mum and Pepper,
and everyone who loves dogs!

Made with love by the team at

FIVE MILE

Five Mile,
the publishing division
of Regency Media
www.fivemile.com.au

Printed in China 5 4 3 2 1

A catalogue record for this book is available from the National Library of Australia

CUTE DOGS

Search and Find Book

By Christie Williams

POOL PARTY

All the dogs are out for a swim, can you spot...

1 Great Dane

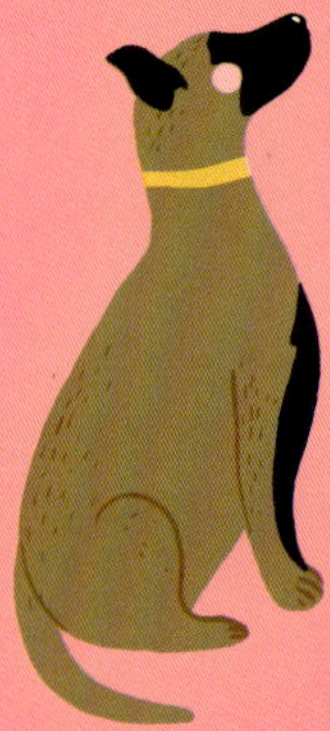

2 Greyhounds

3 Moodles

4 Pugs

5 Butterflies

6 Light globes

EXTRAS!

What was your favourite thing on this page?

Have you ever seen a dog swimming?

Do you like swimming?

PARK

Hiding in the park can you find...

1 Dalmatian

2 Dachshunds

3 Pugs

4 Balls

5 Bones

6 Butterflies

EXTRAS!

How many dogs can you see?

What was your favourite dog on this page?

Do you have a favourite park?

DOG BEACH

The dogs are having fun in the sun. Can you spot...

1 Sand castle

2 Buckets

3 Surfing dogs

4 Beach Balls

5 Balls

6 Pugs

EXTRAS!

Do you like going to the beach?

What is your favourite thing to do at the beach?

How many dogs can you count on this page?

AROUND THE HOUSE

Pug has made a big mess, can you find...

1 Heart slipper

2 Orange shoes

3 Blue sneakers

4 Fluffy slippers

5 Green shoes

6 Purple balls

EXTRAS!

How many dogs can you see?

How many shoes do you see on this page?

What was your favourite dog on this page?

BEDROOM

Scattered around the bedroom can you find...

1 Dalmatian

2 Fluffy white dogs

3 Bones

4 Butterflies

5 Purple toys

6 Stars with rainbows

EXTRAS!

How many dogs can you see?

What was your favourite dog on this page?

If you have a pet dog does it sleep inside or outside?

LIVING ROOM

Now in the living room can you find...

1 Pug

2 Dachshunds

3 Open books

4 Stars with rainbows

5 Stripy balls

6 Bones

EXTRAS!

How many books can you see?

How many dogs can you see?

What was your favourite thing on this page?

BATHROOM

Between the bubbles can you see...

1 Dog shampoo

2 Bubble bath wash

3 Fluffy white dogs

4 Yellow soap bars

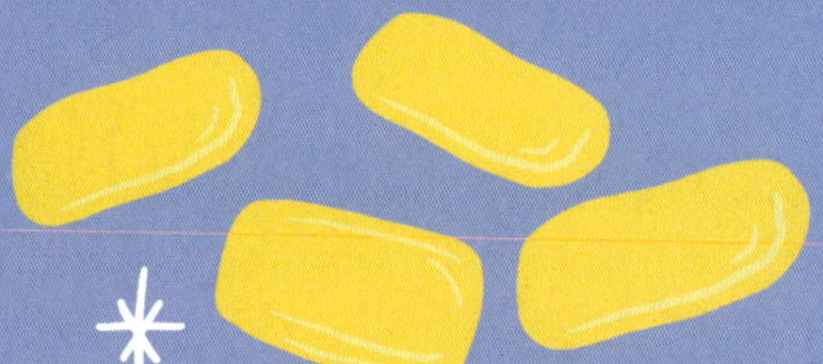

5 Pink bubbles

6 Duck toys

EXTRAS!

How many lilac bubbles can you count?

How many light blue bubbles can you count?

Do you think it would be messy to wash a dog?

BUBBLE
BUBBLE
DOG SHAMPOO
DOG SOAP

BACKYARD

In the garden can you spot...

1 Dalmatian

2 Pugs

3 White fluffy dogs

4 Golden Retrievers

5 Butterflies

6 Bones

EXTRAS!

How many flowers can you count?

How many dogs can you count?

What was your favourite dog on this page?

DID YOU FIND EVERYTHING?

Pool Party

Park

Bedroom

Living Room

WHICH WAS YOUR FAVOURITE PAGE?

Dog Beach

Around the House

Bathroom

Backyard

CUTE DOGS

TOM
DACHSHUND

MAX
GOLDEN RETRIEVER

TILLY
DALMATIAN

CHARLIE
BORDER COLLIE

PUG
PUG

MILO
MALTESE

QUESTION TIME!

WHICH CUTE DOG IS YOUR FAVOURITE?

DO YOU HAVE A DOG AT HOME?

DID YOU SPOT THEM ALL?

ALFIE
COCKER SPANIEL

LUNA
GREYHOUND

BEAR
GREAT DANE

DISCO
MOODLE

FLUFFY
SAMOYED

DAISY
WHIPPET

QUESTION TIME!

WHAT'S YOUR FAVOURITE DOG NAME?

WHAT'S THE LONGEST DOG NAME YOU CAN MAKE UP?

About the illustrator

Christie is an Australian illustrator and surface pattern designer from the Dandenong Ranges, Australia. She specialises in drawing colourful illustrations and especially loves to draw flowers, birds, and cakes. Her work mixes traditional drawing methods with digital techniques to create vibrant colour filled designs. Christie has been professionally designing for over 10 years, with her artwork featuring on fabric, gifts and homewares, apparel, greeting cards, and now books. When she's not drawing she loves spending time reading, exploring nature, and pet sitting dogs for her friends and family.

More books by Christie:

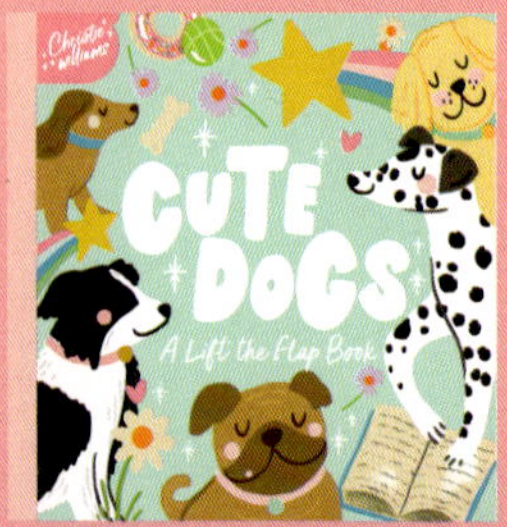

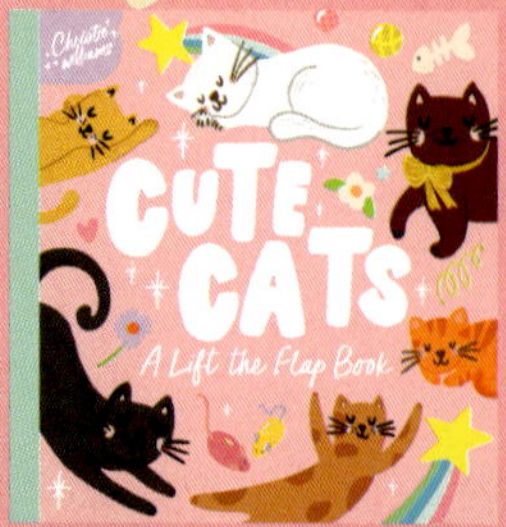

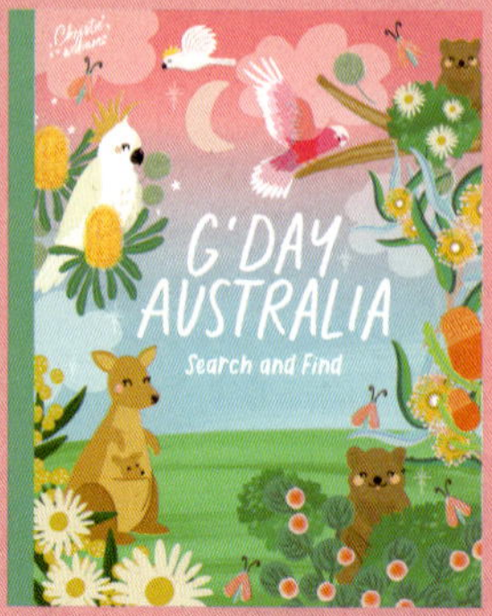